I0417086

This book is not a humorous essay. It is designed to inform Ugandans and most Africans whose countries dictators lead. The book explains proper execution of coup d'état. In this book, you will find concrete ways to topple any African government such as Uganda. I will also explain other aggressive methods to topple any dictatorship whether be Uganda or any other country.

I. Before you begin to think toppling the Uganda Government

Subjugation of a nation is a tremendous undertaking requiring foresight, ingenuity, and careful thought. The first task of many is to decide whether the country is a suitable candidate for a drastic and sudden change in government. The degree of difficulty varies with size, population, political awareness, and literacy. Looking at Uganda as a country, I think it is fair to topple Ugandan government. For the last 30 years, Ugandan people have been subjected to corruption, torture, brutal arrests, murder, poor social service delivery such as poor health facilities, schools, lack of drinkable water, hunger, electricity to mention but a few.

To topple Ugandan government, you need to first differentiate what Uganda is. Whether it is a large state or a small state. A large state tends to contain a greater number of persons, it differs substantially from the small state in that the body politic is much more complex and hence more difficult to seize control of. It is generally advisable to tackle a smaller, unimportant regime rather than a country that, if seized, might draw a foreign power into the coup hence rendering it a failure.

To topple Uganda government, one thing to do before attempting anything of this kind is to make sure you know who your friends and allies are. With a little effort, it is possible to gain a mass of supporters such that it is quite difficult to quell your actions. A way to do this is to select (if possible) a nation whose government does not have support of all of its classes (poor, rich, middle) such as Burundi. Or, if necessary, lure to your cause a religious minority, or ethnic minority, that already has grievances against the current regime. Perhaps you might form a coalition. Summarizing, it is a requisite to get at least some support besides from soldiers of fortune, who are generally "gung-ho" incompetents anyway.

In Uganda, the best candidates to spear head the overthrow can be people like Ret. Gen Muntu, Hon Amama, Besigye and other opposition members. These members need to understand that an okay from USA or Russia is not important because these countries already know what is happening in Uganda.

II. The Mechanism of the Coup d'état

The first thing that should be done is the neutralization of all relevant political forces, including the general infrastructure of the state. This includes, among other things, highways, telecommunications facilities (including radio, TV, etc.), airports, and so on. For Uganda, it is important to know which stations are pro-current government and those that are not. These are political forces controlled by nonmilitary portions of the state (in the event you were wondering). Unfortunately, these are a large and spread apart group of targets, so if you have no tactical or popular support your attempts will be fruitless.

Undoubtedly the absolute first thing you should do is to cut all forms of communications with the outside world off at once. Be sure to include: Telephone, Telex, Wireless, Radio, and Internet etc. THIS IS MOST IMPORTANT. It will prevent the present government from mobilizing its forces, deploying their forces in strategic locations that are not normally guarded, etc. It will also prevent them from calling outside for emergency help, jeopardizing your hard work, not to mention your life. Soon the rest of the world will know something has happened, but they will not know who has taken the government, how the coup is progressing, and so forth. Make sure all forms of communications are completely cut.

One other important thing to do is remove air facilities from the use of the loyalist forces. Close Entebbe airport. A bomb or two in the middle of the runways will do nicely, or perhaps a couple of cars parked there, with snipers preventing their removal. You should not rely on airfields for your coup; if you rely on them and they are shut down, you will encounter problems. The old government will probably rely on them, and you will easily be able to prevent their usage of them.

At an early time during the coup it should be evident as to its success. Uganda government officials and employees of higher rank have a choice to make– whether to remain loyal to the old government, or to join the new attempt at government. If they stay loyal, they may be richly rewarded; if they defect, and the coup fails, they will be out of a job mighty quick. The success of your coup depends much on whether many of these officials decide to join the coup.

In addition to those people who remain loyal and those who join your cause, there is a "wait and see" element involved. Often this is the majority of the population, especially if the present regime is somewhat repressive. They don't want to show too much enthusiasm for either side, until it is more or less decided who gains control. It's best to plan a sudden, abrupt seizure of all facilities to make the coup seem a smashing success; if this is done, the undecided will know to whom to turn.

When you take power from Ugandan government, it is best to know who actually runs it. In Uganda there are three governments: 1- a largely ceremonial government (parliament), the part that people see on television and at most public events. They are, for the most part, what is known as a "figurehead", set off to the side to keep the government's "alter-ego" working on policy. 2- the "real" government, the government that formulates domestic and foreign policy, makes all executive decisions, and basically controls the infrastructure of the nation. The part of the government you will need to take is (obviously) the latter. It is composed of the executive head (Museveni), ministers, and various deputies and second ministers who make small yet influential decisions. 3. Is the judiciary, which is merely a "Museveni" made.

The people you are most interested in detaining (or bumping off) are the Minister of the Interior Gen Nyakirima, the party leaders all the Lumumba, Anites, NRM CEC, NEC members, the Minister of Defense, commanders of Museveni created special forces and the central figure of the "real" government. Once these people are neutralized, in one way or another, the basic functions of the state will be under your command, at least temporarily.

What is often done is to detain (under house arrest, of course) the aforementioned officials, and leave the ceremonial portion of the government alone. This is done to give way for legitimacy and continuity after such an abrupt turn of events. Later, these may be kept or allowed/forced to leave, as need arises.

You will not stay in power for long if you do not exert some sort of influence over the armed forces. The military has the ability to remove virtually any threat if perceives from within the boundaries of the nation. You as a person will cease to exist, unless you leave the country. And, always have several prepared escape routes planned out in advance– even the perfect coup d'etat will have its complications, and there will be things that you have overlooked. That is why it is best to have thoroughly studied the past and recent history of that state. Do your homework! If you do you will be richly rewarded.

III. After the Coup

Once you have removed the major functions of the Ugandan government and bureaucracy from the Loyalist government, you will not yet be in solid control of them yourself. You will want to retain your control, and thus prevent a counter-coup from ensuing. Your new regime will be weakest at this time, and many times some other group seizes the reins of government hours after a coup d'état and this group is not necessarily the old loyalists. The military, political forces within the nation, and the public must all be satisfied to some extent in order for you to continue your rule. This can be attained either by a show of force, or by concessions made to any of these groups, such as a democratically elected government in the near future, or granting the military more influence over political decisions, and perhaps quickly promoting a number of young officers that proved faithful during the crisis. "Promote" those officers who have clout but you suspect might try to take more power for themselves to desk jobs, or remote outposts. And give them all pay raises, if at all possible.

The goal of the new regime is to "shear" off the top layer of government, and more or less retain the old bureaucracy. Lower officials should be made to feel as if little or no change has taken place, and whatever change has occurred is for the better. After a short while these people will realize that the new government is fully in control, and all will be calm and orderly.

Mass media will act as a vehicle to assert your control. Write the first communiqué as a positive, necessary step for a long-needed change. Reassure the people that the coup is a revolt for the masses– not inspired by communists, or an extremist group, but by the public in general. Display the national symbols, and inspire the feeling of patriotism and unity. These techniques were used quite successfully so recently in the 1985 coup d'état in the Sudan. People poured into the streets, waving the old flag of the country, and having an all-around good time. A popular general was instated as the new chief of state, and a democratic government was promised.

Lastly, your new regime has to be made to look legitimate in the eyes of the international community. Show evidence of atrocities made by the former government, witnesses, etc. Take positive steps in the direction of popular democracy, promise elections, and invite the foreign (especially American) press into the country to see these steps. Soon the world will forget about your coup, but whenever your country is in the news, they will remember this.

IV. A Final Word

You will probably realize now that the fast, simple coup was actually the result of much swift planning and hard work. The coup is not an easy thing to accomplish– should you be planning one of your own, know what you are doing and be sure to succeed.

Plan B For Toppling Ugandan Government

1. **Assassinations**
   The quickest and easiest way to change leadership in Uganda is by assassinating the dictator and his close colleagues. There are 6 people that if assassinated, it will lead to change in leadership. These include
   - The president (Museveni)
   - His son (commander special forces)
   - Chief of Police (Kale Kayihura)
   - Ministers of defense
   - President's brother (Saleh)
   - Government custodial

   Ugandans need to read study history of great nations. Many nations assassinate bad and good leaders to change governments. There is always sacrifice. All these actions come with repercussions. Anyone involved in these actions might lose his or her life but at the end save a nation from a dictatorship and hopefully create a true a democracy.

It is not impossible, impractical, or immoral to overthrow current Uganda government.

The ideas of what a free society is, or ought to be are pretty well established. For the last 30 years, Uganda has not changed leadership, the country Uganda has remained a third world with lots of human rights violations, corruption etc. Surely, the need to be a great deal of outreach for more people to understand those ideas before they take hold, but the questions of defense, roads, economy, and law, have been answered. The questions that remains, is how to achieve this.

The answer to is the general public's rightful aversion to violence being taken into account, all proposed paths which have gained any sort of traction have attempted to portray themselves as peaceful. The democratic process civil disobedience, peaceful parenting and education. This all sounds very positive, until we realize that these methods are not peaceful, they just predetermine who the victims of the violence will be.

While we vote, disobey, breed, and teach, the State robs, kidnaps, and murders. (Need I mention that the State is also voting, disobeying, breeding, and teaching?) With every moment that this is allowed to continue, the violence gets worse. With modern weaponry being what it is, nuclear, biological, and chemical weapons, it is not beyond the realm of possibility that the next outbreak of State violence could result in the extinction of the human race. Hell, it wouldn't even have to be war, some intern in a biological weapons lab drops a petri dish, doesn't tell his supervisor, and the next thing you know some 'weaponized' virus is turning us into Resident Evil. That's right, not the slow biters of The Walking Dead, but the strong, fast, variety of zombie that isn't stopped by a locked door.

Science fiction humor aside, this is very serious. We all spend a great deal of time talking about freedom, and economics, but the very harsh reality of this struggle is that the survival of our species is not guaranteed, and the greatest threat to it is very plain to see. Mankind may well know extinction, before he knows peace, and it is entirely possible that we are already too late.

I would far prefer to avoid this. So when I hear about "solutions" that permit the problem to persist, I reject them.

Creating True Democracy In Uganda

I really should not have to spell out the problems with the democratic process. We are looking at them. Anything that so dramatically disconnects responsibility from action is bound to result in bloodshed. While most people do not want to participate in violence themselves, they do fantasize about it often enough. So if they can have somebody else commit these horrors on their behalf and at no direct expense to them, they are generally very enthusiastic about it.

Voting is not a new idea, it has happened for hundreds of years in the United States, and for many more centuries around the world. Tweaking that voting system over the course of years to be more inclusive, and shuffling who gets to vote for what and where, has only increased the rate of government expansion.

I could write thousands of words on this subject alone, but for now I will assume you're already an anarchist. For now, let's take the evidence of failure out of the equation, and just say that the problem is a mathematical one. In any of our proposed solutions, the key is getting enough people to agree with the opposition and those who believe in freedom, happiness and justice for all.

After, carrying out assassinations. Make sure that Uganda will never have a president who stays in power over 10 years. Instill this to citizens by teaching it in schools, mentioning it on TV, media and enshrining it in the constitution. Make it treasonable to overstay in power.

Civil Disobedience in Uganda Will NOT Change Anything.

No one rules, if no one obeys. True enough. Civil disobedience, for the purpose of this book being defined as non-compliance with laws until force is brought to bear, has its merits. Its advocates will look at the American civil rights movement, or the struggle for Indian independence, to say what a wonderful non-violent solution these actions are.

In this section, I will use history and examples so that those reading can apply it to any situation such as Uganda.

They ignore the fact that these things were anything but non-violent. In both the American civil rights movement, and the struggle for Indian independence, countless demonstrators were beaten, imprisoned, and murdered. Martin Luther King, and Mahatma Gandhi were both ultimately rewarded for their kindness with assassins bullets through vital organs. All that was accomplished in the way of non-violence was assuring that the demonstrators remained the victims when the violence occurred, empowering aggressors at the expense of victims.

It also isn't really dis-obedience; so much as it is delayed obedience. Governments surely require a very high rate of compliance in order to accomplish their goals, but they have always ultimately gained that compliance with a threat of force. If one disobeys laws, but refuses to deploy defensive force when government agents come to gain their compliance, then the compliance is ultimately gained, and the purpose defeated. This again, is not non-violent; it only empowers the aggressor at the expense of the victim, as evidenced by countless beaten, imprisoned, and dead activists.

There are those who would say that the goal of civil disobedience is to expose the violence inherent in the system, and there is merit to that. On the other hand, why we need good people in prison to expose the violence inherent in the system is beyond my comprehension. The violence is on the television daily. People vote for wars and gleefully worship dead soldiers. Police who rob, assault, kidnap, and murder are hailed as the saviors of mankind.

Exposing the violence inherent in the system is not only redundant but it is counterproductive. When you disobey the law, and law enforcement comes to gain your compliance with force, and you submit, what you actually do is show everybody how effective violence is. Problem: Lawbreaker, Solution: Force. You are assaulted, imprisoned, or murdered, and the rest of society either cheers for your suffering, or fears these penalties being exacted upon them, and in either case, the outcome is compliance.

Still, the advocates of civil disobedience would say, a large enough civil disobedience movement would be unstoppable. So the problem again becomes a mathematical one. This gives civil disobedience a leg up on democracy, in that far fewer than 50% of the population of a given geographic area can render a place ungovernable, simply by failing to comply.

This sort of requires one to set aside a few harsh realities, not the least of which is, this would still result in a great deal of violence. Governments have been known to open fire on crowds of peaceful demonstrators, and since civil disobedience forbids violent resistance, the demonstrators would have to tolerate bullets flying through their vital organs without fighting back. They would have to continue to disobey, even as the man next to them was beaten, hauled off to prison, or murdered. Fear being a powerful motivator, you can imagine very few would remain both defiant and peaceful under those circumstances.

If civil disobedience aims to prevent violent conflicts, it fails the moment the State decides to make it. If the goal is to prevent an insurrection, then it fails the moment demonstrators decide to fight back instead of going to prison and dying. Since neither of these factors is within the control of the advocates of civil disobedience, I'm going to go ahead and write this off as impossible. If someone else would like to write a book quantifying the number of people they think would need to engage in civil disobedience to bring down a government once and for all, I'd be happy to update this book and perhaps even publish it.

This is not to say that civil disobedience is useless. I think there is a great deal of value in the practice in that it sends a powerful message. It just won't bring down a government by itself. This is dedicated to Dr. Kiiza Besigye who has always advocated for civil disobedience.

Education and Peaceful Parenting

I group these two things because they are essentially the same plan. There are advocates of education who might reject peaceful parenting, but there are no advocates of peaceful parenting who would reject education. In either case, these options, if not coupled with democracy, civil disobedience, or violent resistance, purport to solve the problem of the State by outbreeding it essentially.

If everybody understands that violence is not the way to solve problems, then nobody will engage in violence, and the State will simply cease to exist because people will simply cease to participate in it.

While a fine thing to desire, I don't think this is an entirely honest plan. For the State to be bred out of existence would essentially require a 100% conversion rate. Long before your numbers reached 100%, you could vote the system out of existence. Long before that, you would have the numbers for civil disobedience to be effective. Long before that, you would have the numbers to deploy defensive force. Why you would allow the State to survive for centuries while all of these other options opened up simply defy reason.

So what to do? Analysis and opinion to get rid of Uganda dictator

My proposal, and in all honesty, I'm still working out the details, has been to resort to force. For free men and women to forcefully defend themselves against agents of the State. To kill government agents who would otherwise use force against them, until their jobs simply become so dangerous that they seek other lines of work.

Violently Overthrow the Government

Mind you, I'm not speaking of "revolution" as it's typically thought of. Revolution generally tends to involve organized fighting forces taking out strategic targets in an effort to overthrow the government and replace one government with another. Replacing governments has had mixed results throughout history, depending on how you measure things, but the outcome has always been oppression. In the end, a government will either be an elected one, or a dictatorship. We know that we cannot trust our neighbors to elect rulers for us, that is (theoretically) the position that we are in now. So overthrowing an elected government, and then holding an election, really does seem like a terrible waste of blood. A 17th century British monarchy may seem preferable by comparison, but we can look at countries like North Korea to get our measure of liberty in a modern dictatorship, and cross that option off of our list.

No, the goal of overthrow must be to put an end to the State, not shuffle the deck. Admittedly, history provides us with no examples of this, and that is one of the primary criticisms pacifists have to this approach. They will say that violence begets violence, which we must reason with our oppressors, to appeal to their compassion, to suffer their violence for generations to come, until this strategy yields results.

Need to remind you, that their approach has the same problem? Nobody has ever talked down a government. In fact, people have done a lot more talking, breathing, and breeding, than they have done overthrowing of States. So if we are to say that overthrowing governments only leads to the existence of governments, we can just as easily say that since breathing and breeding and talking have all happened more and with the same result, these behaviors are even more to blame.

Lucky for us, we are intelligent enough to understand that correlation is not equal to causation. So let us discard this fallacy to the dustbin of history. What history actually teaches us about force is that, he who is willing and capable of using force, gets what he wants. It teaches us that the victor of a conflict is the side best at using physical force, not the side with the best ideas. In fact, since the best ideas are non-violent ones, bad ideas have a tendency to win out, and hence, global statism in perpetuity. Every successful revolution throughout history, had always intended to set up a new government. We can argue the merits of that until we're blue in the face, I don't like it any more than you do, but the fact that revolutions resulted in governments, only teaches us that the violence accomplished the desired result. If the government itself turned out to be a miserable failure that should come as no surprise to any anarchist, regardless of how said government was instituted.

Since violence has a tendency to win out over non-violence, and good ideas tend to be non-violent ones, this leaves those of us with good ideas in a difficult position. The moral and intellectual superiority of our ideas does nothing to repel aggressors, so our ideas require teeth.

Luckily, libertarianism provides this. The non-aggression principle forbids initiatory force, and provides for defensive use of force to repel it. Even the most ardent advocates of non-violence will acknowledge this on some level. Stefan Molyneux goes so far as to say an anarchist society would have private defense agencies armed with atomic weapons.

Well, if I were setting up some sort of private military defense agency, the first thing I would do is try to figure out how I could most effectively protect my subscribers, for the least possible cost. The first thing that I would note is that nuclear weapons have been the single most effective deterrent to invasion that has ever been invented. Not one single nuclear power has ever been invaded, or threatened with invasion – and so, in a very real sense, there is no bigger "bang for the buck" in terms of defense than a few well-placed nuclear weapons.

Of course he is here saying that the goal of these weapons is as a deterrent, not as a toy to be joyfully lobbed at competing institutions on days ending in "y". But the reason nuclear weapons are a deterrent is because they can and may be used. This is only the most extreme example, any anarchy-capitalist will tell you that they expect there to be armed people in society prepared to defend themselves against aggression. Whether they are your average citizens with a handgun in his belt, or a defense agency hired to patrol a neighborhood with rifles, the reason they have those weapons is so that they can use them to kill aggressors if those aggressors do not respond to warnings.

There should then be no moral question when it comes to using force against State agents. Badges, uniforms, fancy hats, and popularity contests do not grant someone the right to use violence against me. I have the same right to use deadly force against a police officer during a traffic stop, as I do against any masked assailant on the highway. The same thing goes for a defense agency. If one were inclined to offer private protection services, he has no moral obligation to wait until the State abolishes itself to do so. He is perfectly justified in setting up this business and protecting his customers against theft, even if the thief decides to call that theft taxation.

The problem here is necessarily a practical one. Engaging in gunfights with government agents is very scary. You are outnumbered, outgunned, and statistically less likely to have weapons training. Usually it is preferable to pay the extortion, and move on with your life.

On the other hand, paying that fee is hardly practical if you take a step back and look at the big picture. You are paying that fee because a man with a gun told you to. He is going to use that money to buy more guns, and hire more men, and cars to transport them, and radios for them to communicate on. Paying the fee did not repel the threat, it actually made matters worse, and of course, compliance doesn't always equal survival in encounters with government agents.

Every day there is a new story about police killing somebody, for example, "justifiable homicides" alone by law enforcement average approximately 400 per year in the United States, not including that which the State recognizes as murder or manslaughter. Meanwhile, the number of police officers killed in the line of duty is just over 25% of that number, ranging between 100-150 dead officers per year. More people have been killed by police in the United States since 9/11, than there have been American soldiers killed in the war in Iraq. The death penalty, war, conscription, private sector violence driven by economic controls, the list goes on.

And that's just talking about literal death. Personally I don't place an extraordinarily high value on life in a cage, and I shouldn't have to tell you how many innocent people are experiencing just that right now. How many years in prison would you have to face before holding court in the street became an acceptable alternative to surrender? Ask yourself now, because the laws on the books right now provide decades in prison for a litany of victimless crimes, and as leftists pursue bans on everything from weapons to words, this condition will only get worse with time.

I shouldn't have to explain this to anarchists. The State is a threat to your life, whether you resist it or not.

So here's what we know for certain. There is going to be violence, people are going to die, and nothing any of us do is going to prevent this from being the case. The only question is who will be the victim, and who will be the victor? Being perpetually on the receiving end of violence without ever fighting back pretty much makes certain the answer to this question. For all of eternity, the ruling class will thrive and common people will suffer and die if the pacifists have their way. The only alternative is for common people to do violence against agents of the State.

Met with this morbid reality, people understandably get uncomfortable. They spent most of their lives hearing comforting lies from State propagandists, and if they found libertarianism, they were met with more comforting lies from pacifists. To have both paradigms shattered is unthinkable, they literally can't even think about it.

The good news is, this isn't half as bad as it sounds.

We talked earlier about how many people we would need to convince for any given method to succeed in abolishing any given government such as Uganda. The most attractive part of force is that it requires the fewest participants. Uganda government agents are not the brave saviors propaganda makes them out to be, they are cowards for the most part. If met with the reality that going to work today has a considerable likelihood of ending their lives, they will not go to work, and the government will cease to be.

Let us assume that the average cop writes 10 traffic tickets per day. If 5% of the population of a given geographic area simply understood that force was necessary and proper, a police officer would be coming into contact with one of those people roughly every other day. Up that number to 10%, or be in a place where police write more than 10 tickets a day, and the likelihood of such an encounter becomes much greater. Keep in mind that there is generally more than one police officer in a given jurisdiction.

This very quickly leads to many dead and wounded police in a very short period of time. The news coverage of the phenomenon would be non-stop. If someone you loved were a police officer, would you encourage him or her to go to work under these conditions? If you did show up to work, would you be anxious to answer calls, or make traffic stops? Of course no Police go to work for the same reason all of us go to work, to get paid. If your job means certain death in a matter of days, that sort of defeats the purpose of your paycheck; you're not going to do it. You're no longer at the top of the food chain; it makes more sense to work elsewhere.

If police won't come to work, then how are taxes going to get collected? How are fines going to be issued? How are the edicts of politicians to be enforced? Who is going to pay the town clerk? Simply put, the whole thing comes to a grinding halt once the enforcers decide productivity beats oppression as a career choice.

Of course, there are objections to this. Such as;

"If you shoot at police, the police will kill you!"

There is certainly a risk of this, but as previously stated, that risk doesn't go away by not shooting the cop. More importantly, it is important for people to understand that the winners of gun battles are decided by who shoots first, not who wears what uniform. Losing a gunfight with a police officer is not a foregone conclusion. With a little weapons training, you can easily defeat some lazy bully any day of the week.

"But if people start killing police, then there will be more police!"

Basic math suggests that dead police means fewer police, this is subtraction, and you're thinking addition. For sure, if one police dies, the Ugandan government will just pick from the long line of people who want to be police officers and hire new ones. This is why I'm not out shooting police right now. There first needs to be a critical mass if you will, of people who understand that force is necessary and proper. The idea here is for many dead and wounded police in a very short period of time, within a given geographic area, to demoralize them into quitting their jobs.

"But people will still believe in the Government even after you bring it down, and then they will just erect a new government, and that might be worse!"

Unlikely. Besides, if the enforcers wouldn't show up for work for one government, why would they show up for work for another? We are not revolutionaries trying to replace the British crown, we are people who are fucking sick of being abused and we aren't going to take it anymore. Go ahead and hold your election, when your enforcers abuse us we will kill them and it doesn't matter what 95% of you vote for if 5% of us will shoot back, and by the way, once people see that shooting back works, you can bet the number will be greater than 5%. In the absence of a functioning government, those who were once so infatuated with the government will have no choice but to learn to live without it. Screw convincing them, they will simply have to get used to the idea.

"The public will view you as terrorists!" COMMON TERM

Let them. One man's terrorist is another man's freedom fighter. That has always been, and always will be, the case. Who the terrorists are and who the good guys are is a thing sorted out by history through body counts. For example many people were all raised to believe that the "founding fathers of United States Of America" were wonderful men, despite their slave raping hypocritical behavior. That's because they won the war. If they had lost the war they would have gone down in history as violent terrorists.

"But the Dictator has the army (UPDF and SPC led by his son)"

This is what I can say. In one sentence just ASSASSINATE THE MENTIONED. The problem will be solved

Conclusion

This is my first attempt to write a definitive explanation of my theory on this, I'm sure there will be no shortage of objections to it and I'll take them all into consideration for a follow up. For now, I believe I've made the case that it is not impractical, immoral, or impossible to violently overthrow the government, and that contrary to popular belief, it can lead to a permanently stateless society. Whether or not that ever happens, well, that's not entirely up to me.

What is certain is that the government is a force for bad, and the more time that is allowed to pass, the worse it gets. Most of the world already has very strict gun control laws in place.

Having studied the techniques of the CIA and related organizations, I am pleased to announce the following simple steps in overthrowing a government not forgetting that the quickest way to change Uganda government before 2016 is through assassination.

1. Find some opposition...ANY opposition in the country. Your best bet is some rich members of a former oligarchy or former military. Begin giving them funds, and, start training some of them in case you need to move in the direction of military action. I understand there is a nice training facility in the Florida Everglades that is available as all the Haitian death-squanders who trained there are now busy destroying Haiti.

2. Come up with some reasons that the current government must go. The reasons could be true or not, that is irrelevant. A popular one to use would be economic issue, which goes well with number 4, below.

3. Buy and/or infiltrate significant media outlets. Use these outlets to whip up a broader backlash against the leaders.

4. Meanwhile, use overt and covert means to destabilize the economy. In Haiti, Bush simply held back 500 million dollars in aid already earmarked for that country. There are other ways to destabilize currency, including working with rich elites within the country who will be happy to help. A last resort would be an actual embargo of the country, though that's a tad obvious. Still, most Americans won't notice. U.S had economic sanctions on Iraq for over 12 years and yet when the second Gulf Massacre ended, news media were still talking about how Saddam had ruined the economy.

5. Infiltrate some unions. You'll need some protesters in the streets. You can pay protesters to come. That's fine.

6. Stage some opposition rallies. If possible, shoot some of the protesters and blame this on the government. This worked well in the first Chavez coup attempt. Obviously, do not tell the protesters of your intentions.

7. Ramp up the anti-government rhetoric from the media outlets you control. Be completely outrageous. Call for demonstrations. Slander government officials. Do whatever it takes. The goal is now not just to spread negative information about the government but also to force a response, such as having one of your outlets shut down. Then, violation of free speech gets added to the list of grievances. You can then have some "moderates" come along and say, "Well, I wasn't really that sympathetic to the opposition, but when the government began shutting down opposition media, I realized (insert name of leader here) had to go." If you need to, pay some moderates to say this. This is primarily for U.S. consumption anyway.

8. Go to the CIA Rolodex, and find out whom the Agency controls in domestic media and get them to begin reporting on the opposition movement in ways that make it look legitimate. Be sure these media outlets blame all violence on the current government. The New York Times, FOX and CNN are good places to start. A good example of this in action is the case of Haiti. Despite the fact that the "opposition" are made of U.S. trained former Haitian military and death squads with horrible human rights records, they are called "rebels." Aristide supporters are called "armed thugs." This never fails. Don't worry that some other media will find out the truth and report it. Just make sure your headlines are bigger and get out first. Plant some stories called "The Truth about (insert name of leader here)" and make a lot of shit up. My favorite example was the "voodoo room" they found after they overthrew Noriega. It had "black magic paraphernalia AND drugs".

9. Don't actually kidnap the leader. He should be killed, as was Allende in Chile. Otherwise, they will talk. You see how much trouble Aristide was causing before they found the cell phone someone had slipped him. If it is a Caribbean or African state you are overthrowing, you might want to make sure Reps. Maxine Waters and Charles Rangel are out of the country while it's all going on.

10. Keep your own military involvement to a minimum. Some special forces in local dress is fine, but make sure there is a lot of chaos before sending forces in overtly. Usually, the best approach is to wait until the leader is deposed and then send in "peacekeeping forces." Make sure you wait until the leader is actually deposed, though. It would be awfully embarrassing to be keeping the peace for the leader you are trying to get rid of.

11. Be sure to, at least at first, condemn the coup attempts, as Powell demonstrated in the opening weeks of the Haiti operation. You can switch sides later and no one will question you.

12. It can get messy, but know that, once it's accomplished, any talk that it was a U.S. orchestrated coup becomes a "conspiracy theory" and will be relegated to irrelevant blogs and leftist or conspiracy websites.

Uganda

Background

The colonial boundaries created by Britain to delimit Uganda grouped together a wide range of ethnic groups with different political systems and cultures. These differences prevented the establishment of a working political community after independence was achieved in 1962. The dictatorial regime of Idi AMIN (1971-79) was responsible for the deaths of some 300,000 opponents; guerrilla war and human rights abuses under Milton OBOTE (1980-85) claimed at least another 100,000 lives. The rule of Yoweri

MUSEVENI since 1986 has brought relative stability and economic growth to Uganda. A constitutional referendum in 2005 cancelled a 19-year ban on multi-party politics and lifted term limits.

☐ Location:
East-Central Africa, west of Kenya, east of the Democratic Republic of the Congo

Geographic coordinates:
1 00 N, 32 00 E

Map references:
Africa

Area:
Total: 241,038 sq km
Land: 197,100 sq km
Water: 43,938 sq km

Area - comparative:
Slightly smaller than Oregon

Land boundaries:
Total: 2,729 km
Border countries (5): Democratic Republic of the Congo 877 km, Kenya 814 km, Rwanda 172 km, South Sudan 475 km, Tanzania 391 km

Coastline:
0 km (landlocked)

Maritime claims:
None (landlocked)

Climate:
Tropical; generally rainy with two dry seasons (December to February, June to August); semiarid in northeast

Terrain:
Mostly plateau with rim of mountains

Elevation extremes:
Lowest point: Lake Albert 621 m
Highest point: Margherita Peak on Mount Stanley 5,110 m

Natural resources:
Copper, cobalt, hydropower, limestone, salt, arable land, gold

Land use:
Agricultural land: 71.2%
Arable land 34.3%; permanent crops 11.3%; permanent pasture 25.6%
Forest: 14.5%
Other: 14.3% (2011 est.)

Irrigated land:
144.2 sq. km (2010)

Total renewable water resources:
66 cu km (2011)

Freshwater withdrawal (domestic/industrial/agricultural):
Total: 0.32 cu km/yr (41%/16%/43%)
Per capita: 12.31 cu m/yr (2005)

Natural hazards:
NA

Environment - current issues:
Draining of wetlands for agricultural use; deforestation; overgrazing; soil erosion; water hyacinth infestation in Lake Victoria; widespread poaching

Environment - international agreements:
Party to: Biodiversity, Climate Change, Climate Change-Kyoto Protocol, Desertification, Endangered Species, Hazardous Wastes, Law of the Sea, Marine Life Conservation, Ozone Layer Protection, Wetlands
Signed, but not ratified: Environmental Modification

Geography - note:
Landlocked; fertile, well-watered country with many lakes and rivers

Nationality:
noun: Ugandan(s)
adjective: Ugandan

Ethnic groups:
Baganda 16.9%, Banyankole 9.5%, Basoga 8.4%, Bakiga 6.9%, Iteso 6.4%, Langi 6.1%, Acholi 4.7%, Bagisu 4.6%, Lugbara 4.2%, Bunyoro 2.7%, other 29.6% (2002 census)

Languages:
English (official national language, taught in grade schools, used in courts of law and by most newspapers and some radio broadcasts), Ganda or Luganda (most widely used of the Niger-Congo languages, preferred for native language publications in the capital and may be taught in school), other Niger-Congo languages, Nilo-Saharan languages, Swahili, Arabic

Religions:
Roman Catholic 41.9%, Protestant 42% (Anglican 35.9%, Pentecostal 4.6%, Seventh-Day Adventist 1.5%), Muslim 12.1%, other 3.1%, none 0.9% (2002 census)

Population:
35,918,915
note: estimates for this country explicitly take into account the effects of excess mortality due to AIDS; this can result in lower life expectancy, higher infant mortality, higher death rates, lower population growth rates, and changes in the distribution of population by age and sex than would otherwise be expected (July 2014 est.)

Age structure:
0-14 years: 48.7% (male 8,714,354/female 8,765,900)
15-24 years: 21.2% (male 3,775,679/female 3,833,574)
25-54 years: 25.7% (male 4,618,088/female 4,615,616)
55-64 years: 2.4% (male 405,740/female 447,118)
65 years and over: 2.1% (male 327,771/female 415,075) (2014 est.)

population pyramid:

Dependency ratios:
total dependency ratio: 102.4%
youth dependency ratio: 97.5%
elderly dependency ratio: 4.9%
potential support ratio: 20.5% (2014 est.)

Median age:
total: 15.5 years
male: 15.5 years
female: 15.6 years (2014 est.)

Population growth rate:
3.24% (2014 est.)

Birth rate:
44.17 births/1,000 population (2014 est.)

Death rate:
10.97 deaths/1,000 population (2014 est.)

Net migration rate:
-0.76 migrant(s)/1,000 population (2014 est.)

Urbanization:
urban population: 15.8% of total population (2014)
rate of urbanization: 5.43% annual rate of change (2010-15 est.)

Major urban areas - population:
KAMPALA (capital) 1.863 million (2014)

Sex ratio:
at birth: 1.03 male(s)/female
0-14 years: 0.99 male(s)/female
15-24 years: 0.99 male(s)/female
25-54 years: 1 male(s)/female
55-64 years: 0.99 male(s)/female
65 years and over: 0.8 male(s)/female
total population: 0.99 male(s)/female (2014 est.)

19.3
note: median age at first birth among women 20-24 (2011 est.)

Maternal mortality rate:
360 deaths/100,000 live births (2013 est.)

Infant mortality rate:
total: 60.82 deaths/1,000 live births
male: 70.17 deaths/1,000 live births
female: 51.18 deaths/1,000 live births (2014 est.)

Life expectancy at birth:
total population: 54.46 years

male: 53.1 years

female: 55.86 years (2014 est.)

Total fertility rate:

5.97 children born/woman (2014 est.)

Contraceptive prevalence rate:

30% (2011)

Health expenditures:

9.8% of GDP (2013)

Physicians density:

0.12 physicians/1,000 population (2005)

Hospital bed density:

0.5 beds/1,000 population (2010)

Drinking water source:

improved:

urban: 94.8% of population

rural: 71% of population

total: 74.8% of population

unimproved:

urban: 5.2% of population

rural: 29% of population

total: 25.2% of population (2012 est.)

Sanitation facility access:

improved:

urban: 32.8% of population

rural: 34.1% of population

total: 33.9% of population

unimproved:

urban: 67.2% of population

rural: 65.9% of population

total: 66.1% of population (2012 est.)

HIV/AIDS - adult prevalence rate:

7.44% (2013 est.)

HIV/AIDS - people living with HIV/AIDS:

1,561,900 (2013 est.)

HIV/AIDS - deaths:

63,000 (2013 est.)

Major infectious diseases:

degree of risk: very high

food or waterborne diseases: bacterial diarrhea, hepatitis A and E, and typhoid fever

vectorborne diseases: malaria, dengue fever, and trypanosomiasis-Gambiense (African sleeping sickness)

water contact disease: schistosomiasis

animal contact disease: rabies (2013)

Obesity - adult prevalence rate:

3.9% (2014)

Children under the age of 5 years underweight:
14.1% (2011)

Education expenditures:
3.3% of GDP (2012)

Literacy:
definition: age 15 and over can read and write
total population: 78.4%
male: 85.3%
female: 71.5% (2015 est.)

School life expectancy (primary to tertiary education):
total: 10 years
male: 10 years
female: 10 years (2011)

Child labor - children ages 5-14:
total number: 117,266
percentage: 25%
note: data represents children ages 5-17 (2010 est.)

Unemployment, youth ages 15-24:
total: 5.4% (2009 est.)
☐ Hide

Government :: UGANDA

Panel - Expanded

☐ Country name:
conventional long form: Republic of Uganda
conventional short form: Uganda

Government type:
republic

Capital:
name: Kampala
geographic coordinates: 0 19 N, 32 33 E
time difference: UTC+3 (8 hours ahead of Washington, DC, during Standard Time)

Administrative divisions:
111 districts and 1 capital city*; Abim, Adjumani, Agago, Alebtong, Amolatar, Amudat, Amuria, Amuru, Apac, Arua, Budaka, Bududa, Bugiri, Buhweju, Buikwe, Bukedea, Bukomansimbi, Bukwa, Bulambuli, Buliisa, Bundibugyo, Bushenyi, Busia, Butaleja, Butambala, Buvuma, Buyende, Dokolo, Gomba, Gulu, Hoima, Ibanda, Iganga, Isingiro, Jinja, Kaabong, Kabale, Kabarole, Kaberamaido, Kalangala, Kaliro, Kalungu, Kampala*, Kamuli, Kamwenge, Kanungu, Kapchorwa, Kasese, Katakwi, Kayunga, Kibaale, Kiboga, Kibuku, Kiruhura, Kiryandongo, Kisoro, Kitgum, Koboko, Kole, Kotido, Kumi, Kween, Kyankwanzi, Kyegegwa, Kyenjojo, Lamwo, Lira, Luuka, Luwero, Lwengo, Lyantonde, Manafwa, Maracha, Masaka, Masindi, Mayuge, Mbale, Mbarara, Mitooma, Mityana,

Moroto, Moyo, Mpigi, Mubende, Mukono, Nakapiripirit, Nakaseke, Nakasongola, Namayingo, Namutumba, Napak, Nebbi, Ngora, Ntoroko, Ntungamo, Nwoya, Otuke, Oyam, Pader, Pallisa, Rakai, Rubirizi, Rukungiri, Sembabule, Serere, Sheema, Sironko, Soroti, Tororo, Wakiso, Yumbe, Zombo

Independence: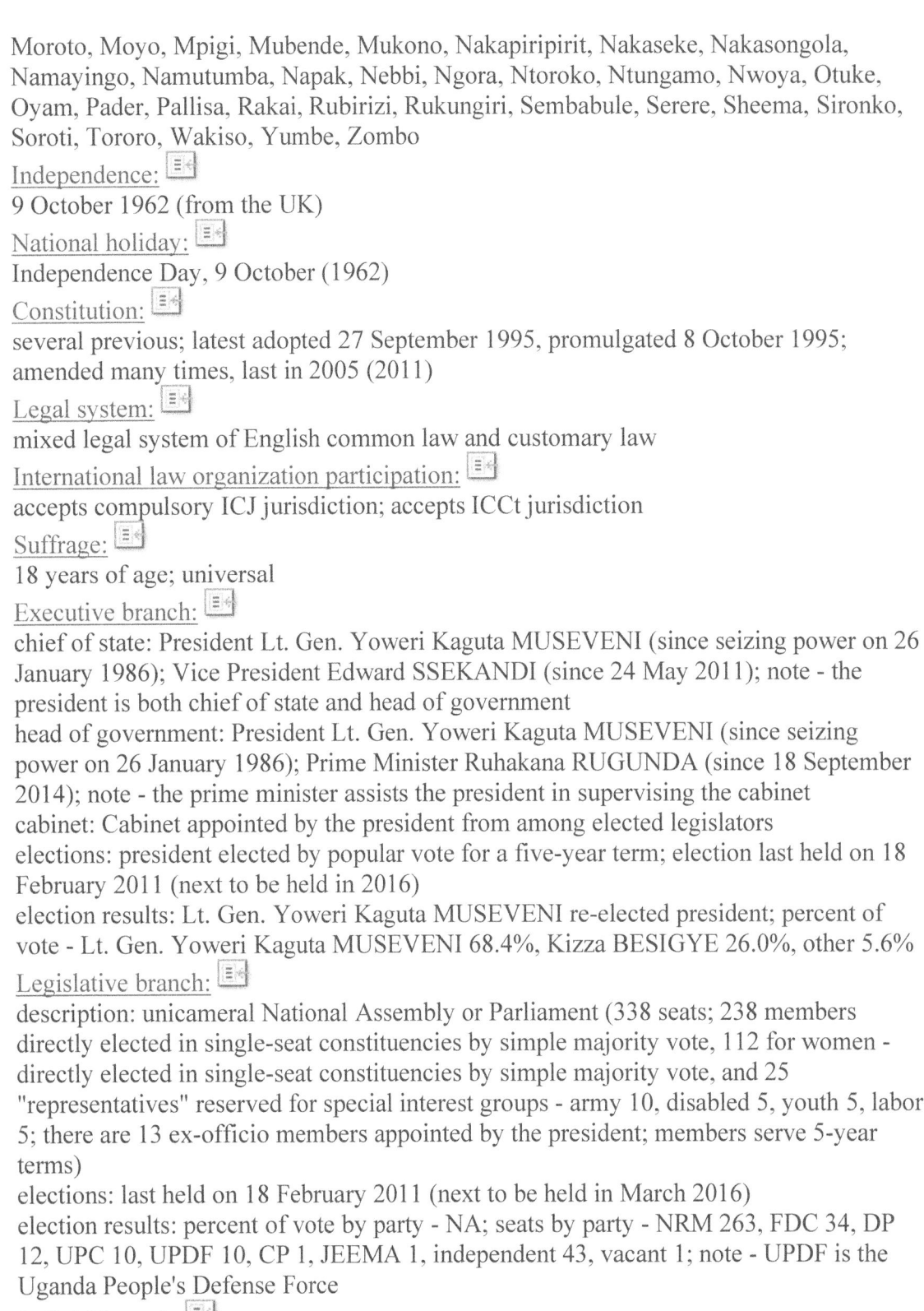
9 October 1962 (from the UK)

National holiday:
Independence Day, 9 October (1962)

Constitution:
several previous; latest adopted 27 September 1995, promulgated 8 October 1995; amended many times, last in 2005 (2011)

Legal system:
mixed legal system of English common law and customary law

International law organization participation:
accepts compulsory ICJ jurisdiction; accepts ICCt jurisdiction

Suffrage:
18 years of age; universal

Executive branch:
chief of state: President Lt. Gen. Yoweri Kaguta MUSEVENI (since seizing power on 26 January 1986); Vice President Edward SSEKANDI (since 24 May 2011); note - the president is both chief of state and head of government
head of government: President Lt. Gen. Yoweri Kaguta MUSEVENI (since seizing power on 26 January 1986); Prime Minister Ruhakana RUGUNDA (since 18 September 2014); note - the prime minister assists the president in supervising the cabinet
cabinet: Cabinet appointed by the president from among elected legislators
elections: president elected by popular vote for a five-year term; election last held on 18 February 2011 (next to be held in 2016)
election results: Lt. Gen. Yoweri Kaguta MUSEVENI re-elected president; percent of vote - Lt. Gen. Yoweri Kaguta MUSEVENI 68.4%, Kizza BESIGYE 26.0%, other 5.6%

Legislative branch:
description: unicameral National Assembly or Parliament (338 seats; 238 members directly elected in single-seat constituencies by simple majority vote, 112 for women - directly elected in single-seat constituencies by simple majority vote, and 25 "representatives" reserved for special interest groups - army 10, disabled 5, youth 5, labor 5; there are 13 ex-officio members appointed by the president; members serve 5-year terms)
elections: last held on 18 February 2011 (next to be held in March 2016)
election results: percent of vote by party - NA; seats by party - NRM 263, FDC 34, DP 12, UPC 10, UPDF 10, CP 1, JEEMA 1, independent 43, vacant 1; note - UPDF is the Uganda People's Defense Force

Judicial branch:
highest court(s): Supreme Court of Uganda (consists of the chief justice and 7 justices)

judge selection and term of office: justices appointed by the president in consultation with the Judicial Service Commission (a 9-member independent advisory body) and with approval of the National Assembly; justices serve until mandatory retirement at age 70
subordinate courts: Court of Appeal (also sits as the Constitutional Court); High Court (includes 10 High Court Circuits and 7 High Court Divisions); Chief Magistrate, Grade One and Grade Two Courts

Political parties and leaders:
Conservative Party or CP [Ken LUKYAMUZI]
Democratic Party or DP [Norbert MAO]
Forum for Democratic Change or FDC [Muntu MUGISHA]
Justice Forum or JEEMA [Asuman BASALIRWA]
National Resistance Movement or NRM [Yoweri MUSEVENI]
Peoples Progressive Party or PPP [Bidandi SSALI]
Ugandan People's Congress or UPC [Olara OTUNNU]

Political pressure groups and leaders:
Activists for Change or A4C
National Association of Women Organizations in Uganda or NAWOU [Florence NEKYON]
Parliamentary Advocacy Forum or PAFO
The Ugandan Coalition for Political Accountability to Women or COPAW

International organization participation:
ACP, AfDB, AU, C, COMESA, EAC, EADB, FAO, G-77, IAEA, IBRD, ICAO, ICC (national committees), ICCt, IDA, IDB, IFAD, IFC, IFRCS, IGAD, ILO, IMF, IMO, Interpol, IOC, IOM, IPU, ISO (correspondent), ITSO, ITU, ITUC (NGOs), MIGA, NAM, OIC, OPCW, PCA, UN, UNCTAD, UNESCO, UNHCR, UNIDO, UNOCI, UNWTO, UPU, WCO, WFTU (NGOs), WHO, WIPO, WMO, WTO

Diplomatic representation in the US:
chief of mission: Ambassador Oliver WONEKHA (since 6 June 2013)
chancery: 5911 16th Street NW, Washington, DC 20011
telephone: [1] (202) 726-7100 through 7102, 0416
FAX: [1] (202) 726-1727

Diplomatic representation from the US:
chief of mission: Ambassador Scott H. DELISI (since 18 July 2012)
embassy: 1577 Ggaba Road, Kampala
mailing address: P. O. Box 7007, Kampala
telephone: [256] (414) 259 791 through 93, 95
FAX: [256] (414) 259-794

Flag description:
six equal horizontal bands of black (top), yellow, red, black, yellow, and red; a white disk is superimposed at the center and depicts a grey crowned crane (the national symbol) facing the hoist side; black symbolizes the African people, yellow sunshine and vitality, red African brotherhood; the crane was the military badge of Ugandan soldiers under the UK

National symbol(s):
grey crowned crane; national colors: black, yellow, red

National anthem:
name: "Oh Uganda, Land of Beauty!"
lyrics/music: George Wilberforce KAKOMOA
note: adopted 1962
☐ Hide

Economy :: UGANDA

Panel - Expanded

☐ Economy - overview:

Uganda has substantial natural resources, including fertile soils, regular rainfall, small deposits of copper, gold, and other minerals, and recently discovered oil. Agriculture is the most important sector of the economy, employing over two-thirds of the work force. Coffee accounts for the bulk of export revenues. Since 1986, the government - with the support of foreign countries and international agencies - has acted to rehabilitate and stabilize the economy by undertaking currency reform, raising producer prices on export crops, increasing prices of petroleum products, and improving civil service wages. The policy changes are especially aimed at dampening inflation and boosting production and export earnings. Since 1990 economic reforms ushered in an era of solid economic growth based on continued investment in infrastructure, improved incentives for production and exports, lower inflation, better domestic security, and the return of exiled Indian-Ugandan entrepreneurs. The global economic downturn hurt Uganda's exports; however, Uganda's GDP growth has largely recovered due to past reforms and sound management of the downturn. Oil revenues and taxes will become a larger source of government funding as oil comes on line in the next few years, although lower oil prices since 2014 and protracted negotiations and legal disputes between the Ugandan government and oil companies may prove a stumbling block to further exploration and development. Instability in South Sudan is a risk for the Ugandan economy because Uganda's main export partner is Sudan, and Uganda is a key destination for Sudanese refugees. Unreliable power, high energy costs, inadequate transportation infrastructure, and corruption inhibit economic development and investor confidence. During 2014 to 2015 the Uganda Shilling depreciated against the dollar, and this, coupled with increased public debt, has severely impeded production, especially since Uganda is a importer of capital goods.

GDP (purchasing power parity):
$66.65 billion (2014 est.)
$62.93 billion (2013 est.)
$59.51 billion (2012 est.)
note: data are in 2014 US dollars

GDP (official exchange rate):
$26.09 billion (2014 est.)

GDP - real growth rate:
5.9% (2014 est.)
4.7% (2013 est.)
3.6% (2012 est.)

GDP - per capita (PPP):
$1,800 (2014 est.)
$1,700 (2013 est.)
$1,700 (2012 est.)
note: data are in 2013 US dollars
country comparison to the world: 206

Gross national saving:
15.1% of GDP (2014 est.)
15.5% of GDP (2013 est.)
15.8% of GDP (2012 est.)

GDP - composition, by end use:
household consumption: 78.9%
government consumption: 8.8%
investment in fixed capital: 24.2%
investment in inventories: 0.2%
exports of goods and services: 21%
imports of goods and services: -33.2%
(2014 est.)

GDP - composition, by sector of origin:
agriculture: 21.9%
industry: 26.7%
services: 51.3% (2014 est.)

Agriculture - products:
coffee, tea, cotton, tobacco, cassava (manioc, tapioca), potatoes, corn, millet, pulses, cut
flowers; beef, goat meat, milk, poultry

Industries:
sugar, brewing, tobacco, cotton textiles; cement, steel production

Industrial production growth rate:
5% (2014 est.)

Labor force:
18 million (2014 est.)

Labor force - by occupation:
agriculture: 82%
industry: 5%
services: 13% (1999 est.)

Unemployment rate:
NA%

Population below poverty line:
19.7% (2013 est.)

Household income or consumption by percentage share:
lowest 10%: 2.4%
highest 10%: 36.1% (2009 est.)

Distribution of family income - Gini index:

39.5 (2013)

45.7 (2002)

Budget:

revenues: $3.434 billion

expenditures: $4.431 billion (2014 est.)

Taxes and other revenues:

13.2% of GDP (2014 est.)

Budget surplus (+) or deficit (-):

-3.8% of GDP (2014 est.)

Public debt:

35.7% of GDP (2014 est.)

34.2% of GDP (2013 est.)

Fiscal year:

1 July - 30 June

Inflation rate (consumer prices):

4.3% (2014 est.)

5.5% (2013 est.)

Central bank discount rate:

14% (December 2014)

14.5% (31 December 2013)

Commercial bank prime lending rate:

20.7% (31 December 2014 est.)

22% (31 December 2013 est.)

Stock of narrow money:

$2.451 billion (31 December 2014 est.)

$2.218 billion (31 December 2013 est.)

Stock of broad money:

$4.262 billion (31 December 2014 est.)

$3.705 billion (31 December 2013 est.)

Stock of domestic credit:

$3.777 billion (31 December 2014 est.)

$3.332 billion (31 December 2013 est.)

Market value of publicly traded shares:

$7.294 billion (31 December 2012 est.)

$7.727 billion (31 December 2011)

$1.788 billion (31 December 2011 est.)

Current account balance:

$-2.224 billion (2014 est.)

$-1.696 billion (2013 est.)

Exports:

$2.66 billion (2014 est.)

$2.829 billion (2013 est.)

Exports - commodities:

coffee, fish and fish products, tea, cotton, flowers, horticultural products; gold

Exports - partners:

UAE 10.9%, Rwanda 10.3%, Kenya 9.4%, Democratic Republic of the Congo 9.4%, Germany 6.1%, Netherlands 5.4%, Italy 4.4%, Belgium 4.3% (2013)

Imports:

$4.714 billion (2014 est.)

$4.512 billion (2013 est.)

Imports - commodities:

capital equipment, vehicles, petroleum, medical supplies; cereals

Imports - partners:

Kenya 19.4%, UAE 14.1%, India 12.2%, China 10.7% (2013)

Reserves of foreign exchange and gold:

$3.246 billion (31 December 2014 est.)

$3.122 billion (31 December 2013 est.)

note: excludes gold

Debt - external:

$4.095 billion (31 December 2014 est.)

$3.594 billion (31 December 2013 est.)

Stock of direct foreign investment - at home:

$NA

Stock of direct foreign investment - abroad:

$NA

Exchange rates:

Ugandan shillings (UGX) per US dollar -

2,600.3 (2014 est.)

2,586.5 (2013 est.)

2,505.6 (2012 est.)

2,522.8 (2011 est.)

2,177.6 (2010 est.)

☐ Hide

Energy :: UGANDA

Panel - Expanded

☐ Electricity - production:

2.493 billion kWh (2011 est.)

Electricity - consumption:

2.284 billion kWh (2011 est.)

Electricity - exports:

70 million kWh (2011)

Electricity - imports:

36 million kWh (2011 est.)

Electricity - installed generating capacity:

711,400 kW (2014 est.)

Electricity - from fossil fuels: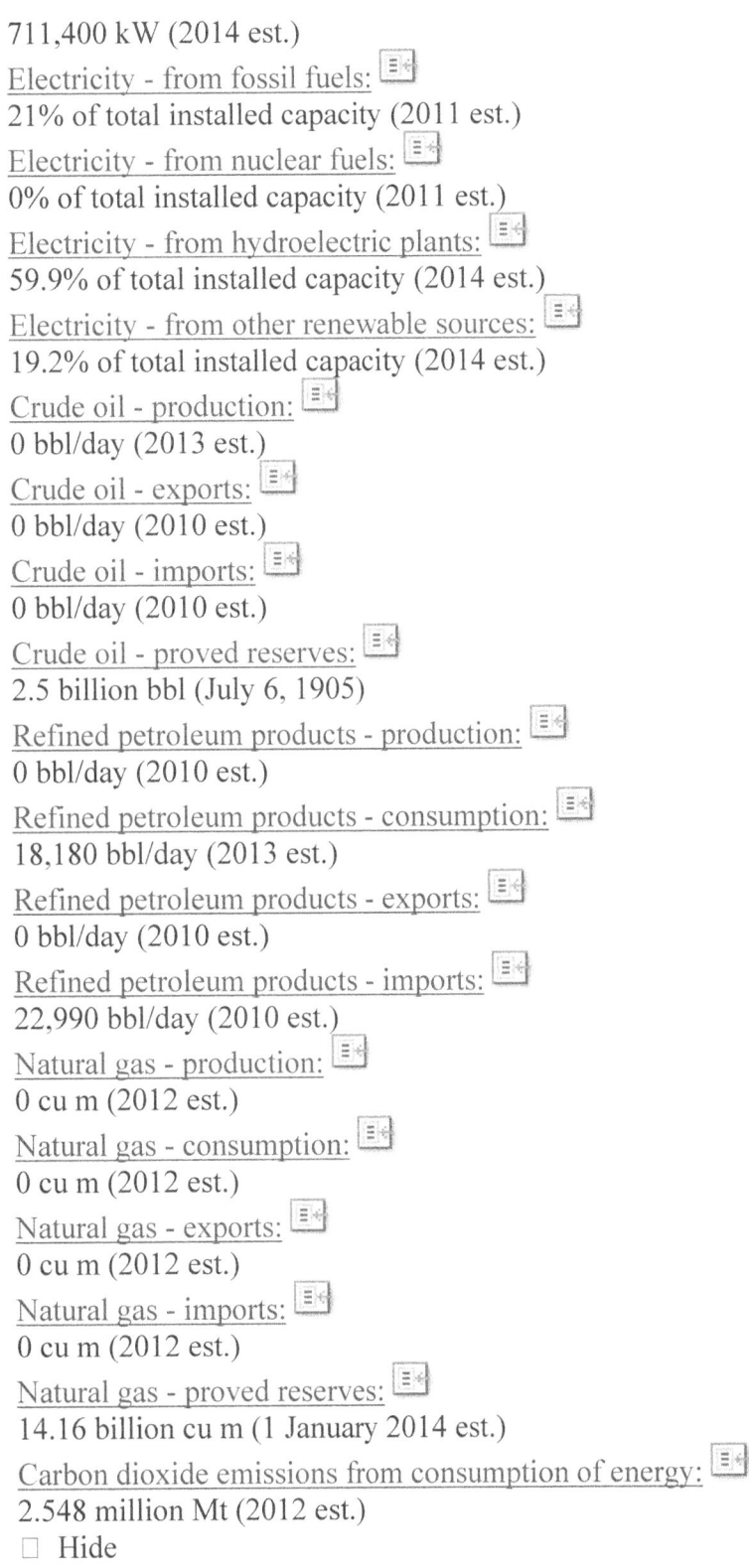
21% of total installed capacity (2011 est.)

Electricity - from nuclear fuels:
0% of total installed capacity (2011 est.)

Electricity - from hydroelectric plants:
59.9% of total installed capacity (2014 est.)

Electricity - from other renewable sources:
19.2% of total installed capacity (2014 est.)

Crude oil - production:
0 bbl/day (2013 est.)

Crude oil - exports:
0 bbl/day (2010 est.)

Crude oil - imports:
0 bbl/day (2010 est.)

Crude oil - proved reserves:
2.5 billion bbl (July 6, 1905)

Refined petroleum products - production:
0 bbl/day (2010 est.)

Refined petroleum products - consumption:
18,180 bbl/day (2013 est.)

Refined petroleum products - exports:
0 bbl/day (2010 est.)

Refined petroleum products - imports:
22,990 bbl/day (2010 est.)

Natural gas - production:
0 cu m (2012 est.)

Natural gas - consumption:
0 cu m (2012 est.)

Natural gas - exports:
0 cu m (2012 est.)

Natural gas - imports:
0 cu m (2012 est.)

Natural gas - proved reserves:
14.16 billion cu m (1 January 2014 est.)

Carbon dioxide emissions from consumption of energy:
2.548 million Mt (2012 est.)

☐ Hide

Communications :: UGANDA

Panel - Expanded

☐ Telephones - main lines in use:
315,000 (2012)

Telephones - mobile cellular:
16.355 million (2012)

Telephone system:
general assessment: mobile cellular service is increasing rapidly, but the number of main lines is still deficient; work underway on a national backbone information and communications technology infrastructure; international phone networks and Internet connectivity provided through satellite and VSAT applications
domestic: intercity traffic by wire, microwave radio relay, and radiotelephone communication stations, fixed and mobile-cellular systems for short-range traffic; mobile-cellular teledensity about 50 per 100 persons in 2010
international: country code - 256; satellite earth stations - 1 Intelsat (Atlantic Ocean) and 1 Inmarsat; analog links to Kenya and Tanzania (2011)

Broadcast media:
public broadcaster, Uganda Broadcasting Corporation (UBC), operates radio and TV networks; Uganda first began licensing privately owned stations in the 1990s; by 2007 there were nearly 150 radio and 35 TV stations, mostly based in and around Kampala; transmissions of multiple international broadcasters are available in Kampala (2007)

Radio broadcast stations:
AM 7, FM 33, shortwave 2 (2001)

Television broadcast stations:
8 (plus 1 repeater) (2001)

Internet country code:
.ug

Internet hosts:
32,683 (2012)

Internet users:
3.2 million (2009)
☐ Hide

Transportation :: UGANDA

Panel - Expanded
☐ Airports:
47 (2013)

Airports - with paved runways:
total: 5
over 3,047 m: 3
1,524 to 2,437 m: 1
914 to 1,523 m: 1 (2013)

Airports - with unpaved runways:
total: 42

over 3,047 m: 1
1,524 to 2,437 m: 8
914 to 1,523 m: 26
under 914 m:
7 (2013)

Railways:
total: 1,244 km
narrow gauge: 1,244 km 1.000-m gauge (2008)

Roadways:
total: 20,000 km (does not include local roads)
paved: 3,264 km
unpaved: 16,736 km (2011)

Waterways:
(there are no long navigable stretches of river in Uganda; parts of the Albert Nile that flow out of Lake Albert in the northwestern part of the country are navigable; several lakes including Lake Victoria and Lake Kyoga have substantial traffic; Lake Albert is navigable along a 200-km stretch from its northern tip to its southern shores) (2011)

Ports and terminals:
lake port(s): Entebbe, Jinja, Port Bell (Lake Victoria)
☐ Hide

Military :: UGANDA

Panel - Expanded
☐ Military branches:
Uganda People's Defense Force (UPDF): Land Forces (includes Marine Unit), Uganda Air Force (2013)

Military service age and obligation:
18-26 years of age for voluntary military duty; 18-30 years of age for professionals; no conscription; 9-year service obligation; the government has stated that while recruitment under 18 years of age could occur with proper consent, "no person under the apparent age of 18 years shall be enrolled in the armed forces"; Ugandan citizenship and secondary education required (2012)

Manpower available for military service:
males age 16-49: 7,249,271
females age 16-49: 7,025,439 (2010 est.)

Manpower fit for military service:
males age 16-49: 4,313,068
females age 16-49: 4,200,901 (2010 est.)

Manpower reaching militarily significant age annually:
male: 423,923
female: 420,236 (2010 est.)

Military expenditures:
2.2% of GDP (2013)

1.45% of GDP (2012)
3.73% of GDP (2011)
1.45% of GDP (2010)
☐ Hide

Transnational Issues :: UGANDA

Panel - Expanded

☐ Disputes - international: 🖻

Uganda is subject to armed fighting among hostile ethnic groups, rebels, armed gangs, militias, and various government forces that extend across its borders; Ugandan refugees as well as members of the Lord's Resistance Army (LRA) seek shelter in southern Sudan and the Democratic Republic of the Congo's Garamba National Park; LRA forces have also attacked Kenyan villages across the border

Refugees and internally displaced persons: 🖻

Refugees (country of origin): 187,838 (Democratic Republic of Congo); 176,398 (South Sudan); 28,005 (Somalia); 16,601 (Rwanda); 14,367 (Burundi) (2015)

IDPs: 30,136 (displaced in northern Uganda because of fighting between government forces and the Lord's Resistance Army; as of 2011, most of the 1.8 million people displaced to IDP camps at the height of the conflict had returned home or resettled, but many had not found durable solutions; intercommunal violence and cattle raids) (2014)

www.ingramcontent.com/pod-product-compliance
Lightning Source LLC
Chambersburg PA
CBHW082246310526
45795CB00015B/3079